TABLE OF CONTENTS

THE ROME OF THE BRAVE

Aaron Bartholome

ISBN-13: 9798332811425
ISBN-10: 1477123456

Cover design by: Art Painter
Library of Congress Control Number: 2018675309
Printed in the United States of America

CONTENTS

1

The sun rose early over Washington, D.C., casting a long shadow of the Washington Monument across the Reflecting Pool and into the Lincoln Memorial, its tip landing like a drawn sword squarely on the 16th President's chest. The cooing of pigeons rang out from the statue and echoed off the stone walls. A light breeze played with the pool's water, causing ripples in every direction. The nation's capital came to life with a burst of energy in the early morning sun.

President Robert Stevens paced back and forth in the White House briefing room, prompting nervous glances from his two Secret Service men standing near the door. He checked his watch, looked up at the clock in the back of the room, then back at his watch. Finally, he went to the window and raised the blinds.

"Sir!" one of the service men yelled, running to block him. "You know that's not safe."

"Right, thank you, Charlie," Stevens said, returning his attention to the stack of note cards sitting neatly in front of his seat. He'd been preparing for this meeting for a long time.

"I just don't want to see anything happen to you," Charlie continued. "Not on my watch, at least."

Stevens chuckled. He couldn't remember the last time he had allowed himself a laugh in recent history. It was certainly a good temporary distraction. But as his cabinet members began to file in, he let out a deep sigh.

He looked intently at the faces of these individuals. The Attorney General. The Defense Secretary. The Secretary of the Treasury. The Secretary of State. Fifteen department heads in all, seating themselves around the conference table and waiting for the urgent briefing they had been assembled to hear.

Stevens took a deep breath.

"First of all, I would like to thank each and every one of you for your expediency in gathering on such short notice. I know that you men and women are busy with your respective duties, and I consider it an honor to work alongside each one of you.

"On that note, however, I must regretfully address the issue of the day. It has come to my attention, through various reputable sources, that there may be a dangerous plot to infiltrate the very fabric of our government, to seize power, to establish a dictatorship and gain sole control over this nation and its hundreds of millions of citizens."

The room instantly became alive with outrage, anger, and panic. Voices echoed loudly off the walls as each Cabinet member tried to shout above the next.

"Sir, you can't be serious!" yelled one member.

"In this day and age? With our strategic security systems?" shouted another.

"The entire government? Impossible!"

The President raised his hand to quiet the noise and addressed Keith Malcolm, the head of Homeland Security.

"Keith, why don't you brief us on what internal intelligence you've collected."

"Well," Keith began, "there's not much else to tell. It's a vague rumor at best. We believe it to be authentic and are treating it as such, but we're still trying to gather more definitive, concrete intel."

"Where's Dan?" asked Michael Bright, the Defense Secretary, referring to Vice President Daniel Sanders.

"The Vice President has already been briefed and has been taken to a secure location in the interests of national security. Additionally, all Congressional department heads and all judicial leaders have taken the necessary precautions as much as possible to ensure their own personal safety as well as to secure the integrity of their respective offices. I would also like to extend to this Cabinet that same opportunity. I myself am leaving the country for an indefinite period. Continue to do your jobs but make every effort to protect your office and protect yourself. Dismissed."

As the department leaders rose from their seats, the President hurried for the double doors, only to be impeded by two secret service men.

"Excuse me, Charlie," he addressed the first man.

"Sorry, Mr. President. I have my orders."

He turned and looked back at his Cabinet standing motionless by their seats, calmly staring at him.

"What is this, some kind of a joke?" he asked. "Did you put them up to this, Keith?"

"No, sir, I did not," the Homeland Secretary replied.

"But you're in on it, though. You all are, aren't you? There really *is* a threat to national security, and it's every one of you!"

"Mr. President, this is for the good of the nation," the Defense Secretary said.

"Really? Kidnapping the president is in the best interests of the people?"

"Yes," Keith said. "Bob, you have no idea what's in store for this nation. Economics, education, agriculture, industry, technology."

"My God," the President said. "How deep does this go? The Senate? The House? Supreme Court? Don't tell me all fifty governors are in on it."

"Nothing as deep as that, Bob," the Defense Secretary explained, "but enough of us to implement lasting change. And our first change is to dissolve the presidency."

Charlie and the other secret service agent grabbed Stevens and escorted him out of the door and down the corridor.

"Where are you taking me?"

"The Oval Office," Keith said. "Our leader wants to see you."

◆ ◆ ◆

There were no empty seats in the large auditorium that morning as leaders from all branches of the military gathered for an important briefing. Most of them knew exactly why they were there; the rest were filled in as they waited patiently for their commander to take the podium.

After a few short minutes, a man in fatigues with a gray-haired crew cut walked across the stage and grabbed the microphone.

"Good morning," the man continued. "As you are all aware, my name is Michael Bright, five-star brigadier general, Secretary of the Defense of the United States, and commander of all military personnel under the banner of the stars and stripes.

"I have assembled here today the leaders of the nation's military forces in order to brief you on the implementation of what we are calling 'Operation: Homefront'. I know that many of you have been briefed on this contingency should the need arise, and I am here to tell you that the need is very real.

"Let me be perfectly clear on this point, though. This is not a police action. This is not an independent move being made by the army to promote recruitment. This is a full-fledged movement with the cooperation of all armed forces to secure the future of these United States.

"We have among us generals, admirals, commandants, captains. It is our duty as servicemen and women to protect our civil liberties at home where they are at most risk. Therefore, toward that end, I am hereby declaring martial law across the entire nation, until such time as a new provisional government may be established. Dismissed."

◆ ◆ ◆

Congressmen Richard Larkin looked nervous as he approached the podium that morning. As Speaker of the House, it was his solemn duty to execute the Congressional agenda and to facilitate any legislation and debate arising from such execution. But never did he have the responsibility that was thrust upon him at that very moment.

"Ladies and gentlemen of the House of Representatives," he began, "I feel it is my obligation to inform you that I am resigning both my office as Speaker and my office as Representative."

Those gathered were abuzz with whispers and murmurs until the forum was filled with noise.

"Furthermore," Larkin shouted, banging his gavel, "I regretfully inform you that each one of you must do the same, in the interests of the nation. The House of Representatives and the Senate are hereby dissolved."

"On whose authority!" shouted a Congresswoman.

Just then, a squadron of Army and Marine personnel marched into the room, their gunsights trained on several Congressmen.

"On the authority," Larkin continued, "of his imperial majesty, the supreme emperor of the United States!"

◆ ◆ ◆

Stevens' heart raced as they neared the Oval Office, and his palms broke out into a cold sweat. Charlie and his partner opened the doors to the office, ushering him in along with his Cabinet. The chair behind the desk faced out the window, hiding the mysterious new leader from view.

"Have a seat," Charlie roughly ordered the President.

As Stevens sat, the desk chair began to slowly turn, until he could finally see who was behind the sinister plot to seize national power.

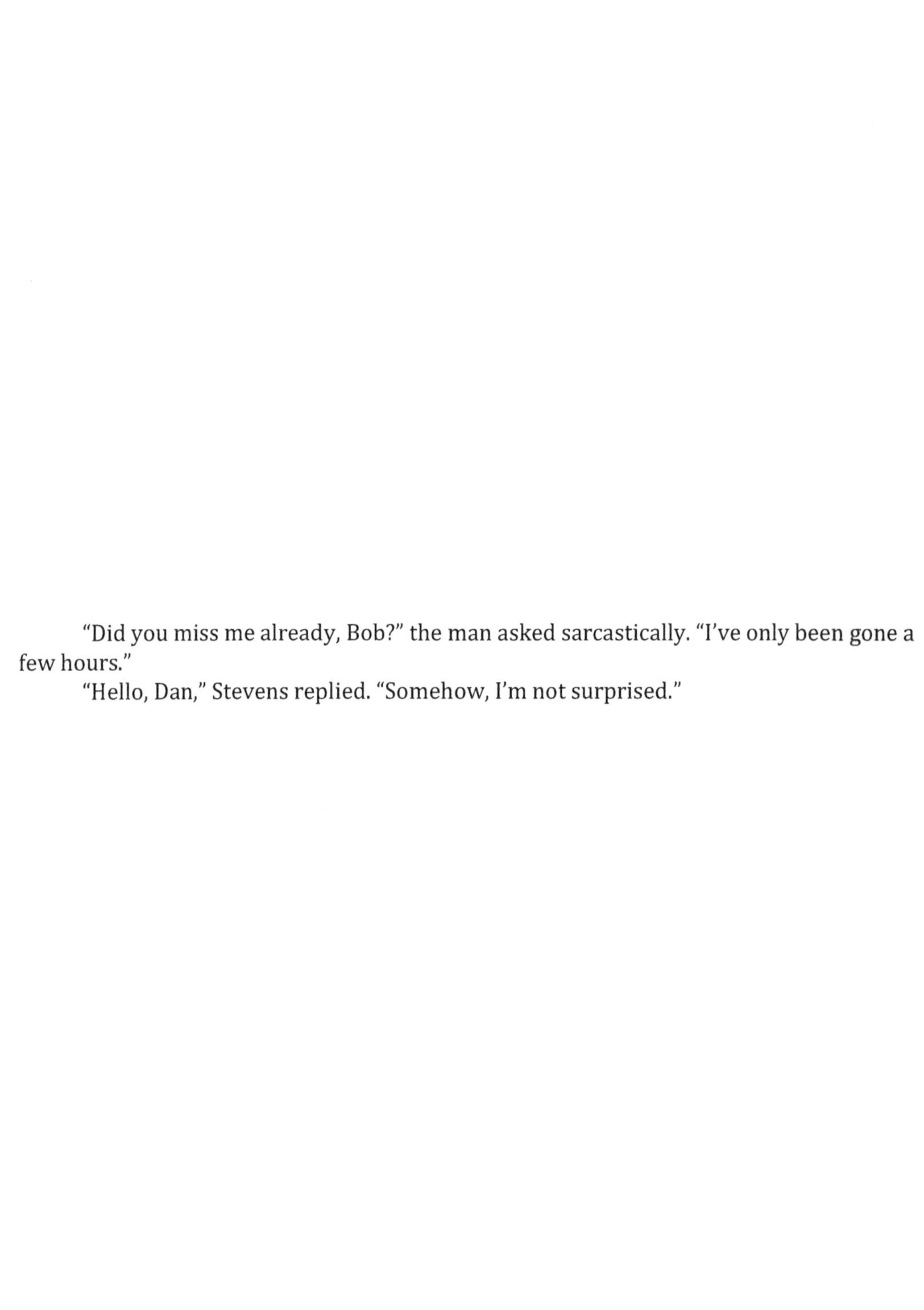

"Did you miss me already, Bob?" the man asked sarcastically. "I've only been gone a few hours."

"Hello, Dan," Stevens replied. "Somehow, I'm not surprised."

2

"You're a madman, Sanders."

Stevens sat across the desk in the Oval Office, staring in the eyes of his Vice President Daniel Sanders, who had just incited a government takeover and assumed the role of dictator.

"This is treason in its highest form," he continued. "Each and every one of you will pay with your lives, I can assure you of that."

He looked around the room, his eyes boring into everyone standing around him. There were four secret service men, the Chief of Staff, and most of the members of the Cabinet, all carrying out Sanders' orders.

"Actually," Sanders said, "this is all perfectly legal and constitutional. Under the 25th Amendment regarding presidential succession, Section 4, paragraph 1 states, and I quote,

'Whenever the Vice President and a majority of either the principal officers of the executive departments or of such other body as Congress may by law provide, transmit to the President pro tempore of the Senate and the Speaker of the House of Representatives their written declaration that the President is unable to discharge the powers and duties of his office, the Vice President shall immediately assume the powers and duties of the office as Acting President.'

"As you can plainly see, Bob, I have the support of your Cabinet, and the Speaker of the House takes his orders from me as well."

"So, you're assuming power by declaring me unfit for duty? You forget the next paragraph of that section, regarding the return of the President by a simple majority in the Senate and House."

"Hmm," Sanders smirked, "I suppose you *could* do that and reclaim the Presidency...that is, if the Senate and the House hadn't already been dissolved."

"The Supreme Court will declare this unconstitutional and have you serving life in Leavenworth!"

"The Supreme Court?" he laughed. "You mean those nine babbling morons that I paid off to leave the bench? *I* am the judge now. You see, Bob, you're outnumbered, and you have no legal recourse. I have won, and from now on you may address me as 'Supreme Emperor of the United States', or – in a pinch – 'Your Highness' will do fine."

"The American people will never go for this," Stevens seethed.

"The American people still think we're hiding aliens in Area 51, a simple nuclear testing facility. They're naïve at best, and they'll swallow any manure so long as we cover it in enough sugar. Now, enough talking. Time to move you into your new quarters."

In one swift movement, the four Secret Service men grabbed Stevens by the arms and escorted him out the door.

"Where are you taking me?" he demanded.

"That, Bob," Sanders chuckled, "is my little secret."

◆ ◆ ◆

The little bell tinkled faintly above the door to Lou's Pub, welcoming its latest patron. A cold breeze found its way into the bar, sending customers diving deeper into their coats and scarves. They all looked up at the man who had just seated himself on a stool and nodded to him in acknowledgement.

"What can I get for you, Brian?" the bartender asked.

"The usual, Lou," Brian replied. "Just make it a single. Times are tough nowadays."

"You doing okay, bud?" asked a man seated beside him.

Brian shook his head, holding his drink in his hands. He looked at the bottles behind the bar and stared off into space.

"Twenty-four years," he said. "For twenty-four years I put my heart and soul into that company, into every vehicle that passed my station, and for what? So they could move and give my job to someone in another country who will work for a fraction of what they paid me."

"That's rough," Lou said. "Your drink's on me tonight."

"Thanks, Lou," Brian said, pulling out his phone. He gazed at the screen, glowing with the image of a woman surrounded by two boys and a girl.

"Now I just have to find a way to tell Becky."

◆ ◆ ◆

"...and so, effective immediately, we are under martial law. This is 'need-to-know', as per the orders of General Bertrand. You will be assigned duties as needs arise and will be instructed at that time. All previous military duties are to be considered null and void as of 1400 hours. Dismissed."

The air on the base was crisp and thin as the battalion filed out of the briefing room. Lt. Col. William Overton stood near the door, saluting and shaking hands as soldiers headed to the barracks to await their new assignments. Two staff sergeants brought up the end of the procession, discussing the change in policy.

"I just don't get it, Chris. I mean, something just doesn't add up about all of this. 'Martial law'? To what extent? County? State? There are only a handful of reasons to declare this, and I haven't heard of anything in recent news to warrant it."

"You know, Johnny," Chris replied, "you're a bit of a loose cannon, and that's what I like about you."

"Thanks, man."

"And it's also what has gotten you into trouble in the past. You'd be in the stockade right now if it wasn't for your dad throwing some weight around. You're an American soldier, Johnny. American soldiers follow orders without question."

"So did the Nazis," Johnny countered. "Look how that turned out."

"I'm sure it's nothing," Chris reassured him. "Probably some racial dispute got out of hand. A couple of weeks on the streets with some Shermans and it'll all blow over. No sweat."

As the two men reached the front of the line, Col. Overton glowered at them.

"Sgt. Jenkins," he said, addressing Chris. "I want no more of your silly pranks or adolescent sense of humor. I don't have to remind you of the gravity of martial law, do I, son?"

"No, sir," Chris smiled. "This is wartime."

"That's what I like to hear," the colonel beamed. "Now, go join your troop and give me a moment with Jonathan, would you?"

"It's no problem, Chris," Johnny assured him. "I'll catch up with you later."

Chris headed out the door to the barracks, leaving the two men alone in the briefing room. Col. Overton quickly scoured the perimeter of the building, making absolutely certain they wouldn't be overheard.

"Sgt. Sanders," he whispered, "your father wants to see you."

◆ ◆ ◆

Stevens jumped as the car door he had been leaning on for hours suddenly swung open. A meaty hand reached in and grabbed him by the arm and, though he was blindfolded, he could tell by the scent that it was Daniel Sanders himself.

"Let's go, Bob," Sanders ordered as he pulled Stevens from the car.

The atmosphere here was calm and a bit on the humid side, unlike the dropping temperatures of early autumn back in New England. The sun shone high overhead, bathing the men in a bright light until just before they made their way through a solid metal door.

Stevens shielded his eyes as he was commanded to remove the blindfold. As his vision began to clear and adjust to his new surroundings, he found himself inside a cavernous metal structure. Fluorescent bulbs illuminated long, winding corridors that seemed to connect the entire facility.

"Where am I?" he demanded.

"Well, now, Bob," Sanders replied with a smirk. "If I told you that, I'd have to kill you, and I'd much rather have a bloodless empire."

"So that's it? You're just going to leave me here alone?"

"Oh, you're not alone."

Stevens looked around him as faces appeared in the corridors, some younger, some older. Most were in business attire and looked rather worn out. At first there were only a few, then a dozen, until finally over 500 men and women were standing in the middle of the large, central structure.

"My God, Dan," Stevens remarked. "You've kidnapped all of Capitol Hill!"

"And the Supreme Court justices, yes," Sanders stated proudly. "Can't have anybody standing in my way now, can I?"

"You can't keep this a secret from the American people. Somebody will notice that their elected Senators are not in session."

"Well, of course I'm not keeping it secret," Sanders replied. "I'm going to formally announce my empirical reign to the American public soon. I just had to 'tie up' some loose ends first."

"And what will become of us?" asked a Senator with a thick southern drawl.

"Don't worry," Sanders assured. "This detention facility has everything you need. Shelter, running water, enough food to last till Doomsday. There's even TV. However, there are no phones, no internet, no wireless signals of any kind, and – last, but not least – no doors or windows. So, play nice, try not to kill each other, and I'll be back to check on you in...let's say...never!"

Sanders pulled a keypad from his pocket and dialed some buttons, opening a false door behind him. As soon as he began to head out, Stevens rushed at him, but instead ran into an invisible wall.

"Oh, I'm sorry," Sanders said, laughing. "Did I neglect to tell you about the force fields? My mistake. Yes, by the way, everyone, there are force fields. Enjoy your stay!"

The false door closed behind Sanders, leaving Stevens, Congress and the Supreme Court abandoned in an unknown facility with no visible means of escape. Stevens looked at his fellow prisoners and sighed.

"What do we do now, Mr. President?" the southern Senator wondered.

"We do exactly what Dan told us to do," he replied, a look of determination on his face. "We start working together."

3

Staff Sergeant Jonathan Sanders stepped out of a green Humvee and onto the White House lawn. There had been no briefing en route as to what this meeting was about, only that his father wished to see him. Since his father had been elected Vice President, however, the few times Johnny had spent with the man were strictly business.

The Secret Service ushered him down the hallway that led to the Oval Office. He had been here before, but each time he passed the portraits on the wall, he gazed at them in awe. Presidents who helped to shape the country into what it is today. And his father was a part of it.

As he entered the Oval Office, he was met with a busy camera crew bustling about. Two men were setting up tripods while others were erecting lighting mounts on either side of the room. Behind the desk sat Sanders, attempting to check his lapel mic while a make-up artist dabbed his face with powder.

"Johnny!" he shouted, shooing away the assistant. "Glad you could make it, son."

Johnny looked at the armed guards to his left and his right.

"I don't know that I had much of a choice. What's all this?"

"A new era, my boy," Sanders said, leaving his desk and embracing his son. "A brand-new regime for the good of America."

"Sorry, dad," Johnny replied, escaping a bear hug, "but the word 'regime' has historically never meant good for anyone but those in power. What's going on?"

"Well, you're looking at the new emperor of America. I have all power and authority over this nation and there is no branch of government to stand in my way."

"Let me get this straight. You staged a successful coup and eliminated the legislative and judicial branches of government?"

"Not 'eliminated'. Just creatively shifted responsibilities. Now the making and interpreting of laws rests squarely on my shoulders. I will delegate as necessary, of course, but ultimately it will be under my authority."

"You're a maniac, dad. This is not how America is to be run. This is not what Washington and Jefferson envisioned."

"No," Sanders said, "this is better. With no one opposing my ideas, I can do what's right for this country. No more debt, no more hunger, no more unemployment. Better education, better health care. Stuff that those goons in the Senate would never pass.

"And how about you? How does the title 'Colonel' appeal to you?"

"Great," Johnny said. "With that name I can make a good living frying chicken."

Sanders returned to his desk, settling in to make his big announcement to the nation.

"Even if you don't agree with me," he told his son, "you can at least stay and watch your old man at work."

"As I said," Johnny replied, looking at the guards, "I don't have much of a choice."

❖ ❖ ❖

Brian Murray stared at his dinner plate, pushing around a mound of mashed potatoes. His daughter, Hayley, sat next to him, texting her friends, while the twins – Ricky and Randy – made walrus faces with their carrots. Becky glanced at her boys with a giggle, then noticed her husband had barely taken a bite.

"How was work today, dear?" she inquired.

"Work? Oh, it was great," he lied, sitting up and looking at his wife.

"Did something happen? You seem a little down."

"Well, yeah…I mean, no…it's just that, the company decided it can make pick-ups a lot cheaper elsewhere…like, Mexico."

"We're moving to Mexico?" Hayley asked, looking up from her phone.

"No, sweetie," Brian replied. "Daddy lost his job."

"Oh, honey," Becky comforted, reaching her hand across the table and grabbing his. "I'm so sorry."

"I just don't know how we're going to survive now."

"We'll make it work, don't worry. God will provide for us. He always has. Besides, I think I may be getting a raise down at the station."

"Oh, that's great," Brian answered. "Did you finally get that 'live-on-the-scene' reporter spot you've been angling for?"

"Not yet," Becky confessed, "but I can smell a good scoop. I know something big is coming soon. I just have to sniff it out."

◆ ◆ ◆

"How should we proceed, Mr. President?"

Robert Stevens was facing a large room full of Senators and Representatives, yet instead of giving them a "State of the Union" address, he was tasked with leading them to work together to find a way out of their current predicament – a solid metal bunker with no visible means of escape.

"Well, first, we should do what we do best."

"Debate along party lines?" someone snickered.

"No," Stevens laughed. "We should form committees, and I think the first ones should follow Maslow's basic need principles. Now, we already have shelter, but I want some of us to arrange sleeping quarters. I also want a committee for food rations, one for hygiene and one for clothing. I want reports every hour.

"Our secondary task is, of course, to find a way out of here. I want those with any scientific or mechanical backgrounds to gather back here at 1600 hours to discuss escape strategies. And let me be abundantly clear – while we are working together, there are no more Democrats, Republicans, Tea Party, Libertarian, or Independents among us. Politics is of little use to us right now. Cooperation for the common good of all is of utmost importance. Dismissed."

Immediately, Congressmen from all walks of life and party platforms set to work on maintaining the basic necessities of life in the bunker, which proved to be extremely effortless, as they had been provided with an overabundance of supplies. Sanders had told them the truth. They had everything they needed to survive.

"Reports from all over the bunker have returned positive thus far, Mr. President," one Senator announced, rubbing his head.

"You okay, Senator?"

"Yes, sir, just a slight headache. Nothing to worry about. As I was saying, I believe we have more than enough to live on in here for another fifty years. But here's hoping we won't have to test that theory out."

As he was giving his report, a Congressman ran through a side corridor toward the President, visibly out of breath.

"Sir," he panted, "we may have a slight problem. It may be nothing."

"You're in an awful big hurry for nothing," Stevens remarked.

"Right, sir. Well, several of the others have been reporting dizziness, nausea and…"

"Headaches," Stevens finished, looking at the first Senator.

"Yes, sir, from Sector 3. How did you know?"

"What sector were you working in, Senator?" he asked the first man.

"3, sir."

"My God," Stevens sighed. "Okay, it sounds localized, but let's not rule out an epidemic. Have everyone who was working there quarantined, and seal off Sector 3. Find out who in this place has any medical experience and assemble a makeshift hospital staff. Top priority."

"Understood, sir," the Congressman replied. "And by the way, sir, I have a bit of medical training myself, and if I didn't know any better, I'd say these are early symptoms of radiation exposure."

◆ ◆ ◆

"What's on the tube, Lou?" asked a man at the bar.

"I think the game's on," Lou replied, flipping the switch on the television. The image of a running back carrying the football over the 10-yard line was immediately interrupted by static.

Meanwhile, every TV set across the nation, regardless of what channel it was currently tuned to, was replaced by a short burst of static, and then the smiling face of the Vice President of the United States.

"My fellow Americans, let me begin by saying how good it is to finally address you personally. I'm sorry to have interrupted your current entertainment of choice, but this is a matter of dire importance for the nation as a whole.

"You see, the reason for my personal address is that there has been some recent 'shake-ups' in Washington. Now, I'm not much for gossip, but I will say that there was a plot to overthrow the government and, in an effort to preserve the solidarity of the union, I authorized martial law and had all those involved in the conspiracy confined to an unknown location. Sadly, this turned out to be most of those on Capitol Hill, including the Senate, House and even the President himself.

"However, we will survive, although there is no Constitutional precedent for a situation such as this. Therefore, in light of this, I have hesitatingly dissolved the legislative and judicial branches of the government until such time as Capitol Hill can be electorally replaced. I alone am now responsible for the welfare of this great nation, a responsibility I don't intend to take lightly. I will rely on the remaining staff I have here in Washington, including Defense Director Michael Bright, Homeland Director Keith Malcolm, and my new Chief of Staff, former House Speaker Richard Larkin.

"I see big changes during my stay in the White House. There will be reforms across the board in terms of economics, education, foreign diplomacy and warfare. I will attempt to rid this country of unemployment, poverty and hunger. But, I need your help, your trust, your confidence. I need your support. Together, we can restore these great United States of America to the glory she once held among the nations of the world. Thank you and good night."

4

"And we're clear!" shouted the director.

Daniel Sanders, the former Vice President who had just declared himself Emperor of the United States to the entire nation, fidgeted in his seat. He loosened his necktie and unbuttoned the top of his shirt, exhaling deeply.

"God, I never liked wearing these things. Rick, what's on the agenda today?" Richard Larkin's phone vibrated in his pocket. Ignoring Sanders, he grabbed it out and saw who was calling – "*Becky*".

"Hello? Hi, sweetheart...no, we haven't lost our minds here...it's just like he said, there had to be a shakeup...we are *not* communist dictators...you know, sometimes you sound just like your mother, God rest her soul...yes, I know you're going to share your side of the story...look, I have to go, but I love you and miss you...give my best to Ben...oh, Brian, right...bye."

"Everything okay, Rick?" Sanders asked.

Larkin looked up from his phone and glanced around the room. All eyes were on him, anticipating his answer.

"Yes, well, I'm good. It was just Becky."

"As in your daughter, Becky? The one who works for Channel 6?"

Larkin exhaled.

"She sounded a bit concerned," he admitted, "and she's a brilliant reporter. We may have a problem."

◆ ◆ ◆

Robert Stevens paced the floor in the great "assembly room" of their metal prison. It had been hours since either of the makeshift teams had reported back with any new developments. On the one hand, there was still no progress made into determining a weakness or exit to the structure, and on the other, men and women were continuing to exhibit symptoms of radiation poisoning. Something had to give soon.

"Sir, I have an idea!" someone shouted down the corridor, walking briskly toward Stevens. It was Congressman Bill Coleman, holding a clipboard.

"Sir, I think I may have found a possible escape."

Stevens halted his steps and pricked up his ears.

"I'm listening, son."

At 30, Coleman certainly wasn't a young boy, but he was the newest elected Representative with barely a year of service under his belt. However, what he lacked in experience, he made up for in other ways. He had graduated from MIT with honors and had been Steven's first choice to head up the science team.

"It involves the force field that Sanders erected when he left," he explained. "I've been analyzing it and making some rough calculations, and I think I know a way to disengage it."

"How is a force field even possible?" Stevens wondered. "I thought that was all sci-fi stuff."

"Well, sir," Coleman replied, "technically, force fields exist in nature quite frequently. They occur whenever forces of equal strength are drawn to one another, creating an invisible field between them, such as gravity, or electrostatic, or magnetism."

"So, Sanders created some sort of electromagnet here to generate a force field? He's no scientist."

"No, sir, he isn't. And he didn't do this. In fact, if my physics professors were right, I'd say this stuff has been here for at least…"

A horrifying scream cut off the Congressman's words as it reverberated through the acoustic chambers. A man came running down the corridor, shouting at the top of his lungs.

"She's gone! She's gone! My God!"

Stevens grabbed the man by the shoulders, containing him.

"What's wrong, Senator? Who's gone?"

"Senator Haskins," he managed. "The sickness…the sickness…my God, she's dead!"

"The radiation!" Stevens yelled, pounding the steel wall. "I want every crevice, nook and cranny within a 100-yard radius of that crap evacuated. No one goes anywhere near it, is that understood?"

The senator looked at the President through tear-soaked eyes and nodded his head, then made his way back to inform the others of the plan. Stevens gruffly returned his attention to Coleman.

"How's that force field coming, Congressman?"

"Well, as I was saying, sir, it should be no problem. I'll just have to sustain it long enough to trace it back to a power source, and then impede the circuit and we'll be home free."

"I don't like it. It sounds too easy."

"Well, it may not be that easy. I mean, from what I can tell this thing has all the earmarks and fingerprints of Nikola Tesla."

"Tesla?" the President asked. "The Serbian physicist responsible for the advancement of weapons and engineering technology for the Axis Powers in WWII?"

"I seriously doubt he helped the Nazis," Coleman chided, "but you know your history. I'm not convinced Tesla installed this himself, though it is consistent with his designs, which would probably put this one at around 70 years ago."

"The 1940's? So, what you're telling me is that there is an electromagnet in an underground, WWII-era bunker that's contaminated with lethal doses of radiation?"

"Apparently so, sir."

"My God," Stevens whispered to himself. "I know exactly where we are."

♦ ♦ ♦

"With News Channel 6, I am Becky Larkin."

"Hey, Becky, can I talk to you for a sec?"

Becky looked in the mirror at the reflection of Bruce Barnes, Channel 6 station manager, standing in the doorway.

"Sure thing, Bruce," she said, smiling and turning toward her boss. "As long as it's not about my assignment."

"It's about your assignment," Bruce confessed, prompting a groan from Becky. "It's not me. It's the higher-ups."

"Bruce, I have the talent, I have the ratings and I have the experience."

"And you also have the same last name," he reminded her. "Look, everyone knows you, and everyone knows that you are Richard Larkin's daughter. We pride ourselves on unbiased journalism, but if you report on the government shakeup, anything you say is going to be scrutinized through the lens of favoritism."

"Maybe I can go by my married name for once; you know – Becky Murray."

"Won't help. People still know you."

"But Bruce…"

"No buts," Bruce demanded. "Peter will take this assignment. I'm giving you the bakery fire."

"Oh, please! Mrs. Peabody is 88 years old. She turned on the stove and forgot all about it. End of story."

"Look, just humor me and stay out of Washington, okay. Any debates between you and your father should not make the five o'clock news. They should be saved for the Thanksgiving dinner table like any normal family."

As Bruce stormed back to his office, Becky walked into the press room.

"Hey, Peter, you busy?" she asked.

"No, I think I got a sec. Just as long as I catch my plane to D.C. in two hours."

"That's what I need to tell you. Umm…well, the flight's been cancelled, so…. yeah, bummer deal, huh?"

"Oh, man, now I'm going to miss my interview with my source."

"Tough break, man," Becky said. "Hey, listen, though. I just had a thought. Why don't you take my bakery fire? I mean, I think Mrs. Peabody said something about hooligans hanging out there recently. Could be a hard-hitting exposé."

"Thanks, Bec, I think I will," Peter replied, heading for the door.

"Don't mention it."

"You know," Peter smiled, turning around, "you have always been a good friend."

"You have no idea," she said, grabbing her phone as he left the office.

"Hello, dad? Yeah, I can be there in less than two hours…I can't wait to see you, too…"

◆ ◆ ◆

Daniel Sanders busied himself in front of the mirror in the Lincoln bedroom. It had been a long day, fielding questions from the press and trying to make the nation understand why the new administration was better for everyone.

"Your pajamas look fine tonight, darling. Just come to bed."

Sanders turned around and stared at the woman lying under the sheets.

"One more moment, sweetie. I have to make sure I'm ready."

"Dear, you haven't been 'ready' since the takeover started. Let's just get some sleep."

Daniel obediently climbed into his side of the bed, grabbing a book from the nightstand.

"You know," he said, "Lincoln died in this room, in this very bed, perhaps. Some say that his spirit still lingers here."

"I say, 'Get some sleep, Emperor'."

"I just wonder, though, you know, if Abraham sees everything that goes on in this house, like a presidential watchman."

"Feeling guilty?"

"Not really," Sanders admitted. "Just wondering how much Robert actually knows."

"He knows all he needs to know. Now good night, Your Highness."

"Good night, First Lady Stevens."

5

"Area 51?"

President Stevens stood at the front of the large open room in the middle of the bunker. His recent discovery of radiation and 1940's technology pointed to one logical conclusion.

"Yes," he said. "I believe that we are being held captive in the facility known as 'Area 51', located in the Mojave Desert in western Nevada. Fortunately, there is a United States Air Force installation here as well – Nellis AFB – and our goal is to escape this bunker and seek their help. Questions?"

"What about the radiation?"

"The radiation is continued fallout from the atomic testing done in this desert during WWII, but the contaminated area has been evacuated and quarantined. There should be no further illnesses."

"How are we supposed to escape this place?"

"Good question," Stevens replied. "I'm going to let the expert field that one. Senator Coleman?"

Bill Coleman stepped in front of his fellow senators with a smile on his face.

"My friends, I have good news. I have found a way to disconnect the electromagnet from the circuit, but only for about five minutes. Which means, once I disrupt the power source, we'll need to be in place and ready to head through."

"What about the main metal door past that?" a woman asked.

"That door also works on the same circuit path. I will hold both open for as long as I can, but I will only be able to buy you a few more seconds at most."

"I realize it's not going to be easy," Stevens explained. "It's a narrow door, and there are a lot of us. But it's our only shot."

"What are we waiting for?" someone yelled. "Let's blow this dump!"

Senator Coleman walked down a corridor and opened a metal panel. Carefully, he pried up an interior plate, exposing a blue energy field.

"You know," he said, looking down the hallway toward Stevens, "this really is a complicated piece of technology. In fact, I've already tried to shut it down, but this field passes through anything I throw at it – except for one specific material."

Stevens drew closer as Senator Coleman held up his left hand. His fingertips were blackened, and a purplish hue ran down to his palm.

"I slipped," Coleman explained. "The beam fluctuated for a brief nanosecond. By my calculations, an entire human body could shut off the grid for about..."

"...five minutes," Stevens finished. "You're not going with us..."

"Someone has to stay behind and turn off the lights. Might as well be me."

"But Senator Haskins is dead already. Could we use her body?"

"Sorry," Coleman answered. "It has to be living, active tissue. Besides, the radioactive isotopes she was exposed to are great conductors of EM energy. No resistance."

Stevens nodded his head, heading back to lead the others out of the bunker.

"Godspeed, Mr. President," Senator Coleman called after him, throwing himself into the heart of the EM matrix.

As the grid shut down, everyone carefully made their way through the giant metal door and out into the bright Nevada sunlight.

◆ ◆ ◆

Becky Murray quickly made her way to the White House for her interview with her father, Richard Larkin, who had just been appointed Chief of Staff by the new, self-proclaimed emperor of the United States. There had been a formal press conference earlier, of course, but being the daughter of a politician always got Becky the best of everything.

The Oval Office was practically empty when she arrived that afternoon. The only people in the meeting were Larkin, Becky, Emperor Sanders and Keith Malcolm, the Director of Homeland Security.

"Good afternoon, gentlemen," she began. "First of all, let me just point out that I am completely objective. Nothing you say will be edited, deleted, exaggerated or added to. That being said, gentlemen, I'm all ears."

"You won't hear anything that hasn't already been said at the press conference," Sanders said gruffly. "Which is nothing more than what I said in my address to the nation. Reliable sources revealed a conspiracy to commit treason by the President and Congress."

"The *entire* Congress? All 535 elected members? And lobbyists? I find that extremely difficult to believe."

"Well," added Larkin, "believe what you want, sweetie, but that's our story, and that's what you're reporting, Mrs. Objectivity."

"And if you're not convinced," Sanders said, "we have videotaped confessions by all parties involved in the treason, including the Supreme Court. Two days' worth of evidence, if you're interested. The other press didn't even get this invitation."

"I suggest, dear," Larkin said, "that you take this opportunity to review all of the facts. I think you're only getting part of the story, and that can be very...*dangerous*."

◆ ◆ ◆

"I just don't get it, Chris. Dad has taken over the whole country and I'm still stuck playing security guard in Nevada."

"Yeah," Chris replied, "but at least we're guarding Area 51. This place is cool, Johnny!"

"This place is off limits," Johnny corrected. "Besides, there are no alien ships or anything like that here. This was simply an atomic testing site in the 1940's, owned by the Department of Energy, and is now the home of Nellis Air Force Base. Nothing too 'cool' about it.

The CO walked into the barracks, interrupting their conversation. He had a rough, mean look on his face today, causing Sanders and Jenkins to give shaking salutes as they stood at attention.

"At ease, gentlemen," the colonel said. "The science and communication labs have shown some unusual glitches in the power grid down at the bunker. Jenkins, you and Sanders are to report there immediately to find out what's going on."

"Oh, but sir," Jenkins stammered, "we're not detectives."

"NOW!" the colonel bellowed.

"Going, sir," Jenkins acknowledged. "Johnny, keep your eyes peeled."

"I told you, Chris, there's nothing here. It's an empty bunker. Probably some squirrel fried itself on a transformer or something."

"All the same buddy, let's be ready for anything."

◆ ◆ ◆

Stevens and his group shielded their faces as their eyes became readjusted to the bright Nevada sun. They had emerged approximately 2 miles from the nearest Air Force barracks, and they began their trek through the heat in order to find shelter.

"All right, everyone stay together. Nellis is just ahead to the west. Once we get there, we'll explain to the CO exactly what has happened, and we're home free."

"What about what Sanders said in his broadcast?" someone asked. "He essentially declared us to be outlaws."

"Don't worry," the President assured. "When we get to base, I expect a full governmental welcome for the lost Congress."

As soon as he spoke, two uniformed men approached the group from the direction of the barracks and aimed their weapons.

"I got a trigger finger, Stevens," the first one said, fixing a red dot on his forehead.

"Put that down, Chris," the other chided him. "You're liable to hurt somebody."

"You're Daniel's son, aren't you?" Stevens inquired.

"Yes, sir, Mr. President," he replied. "Sgt. Jonathan Sanders, US Army, currently stationed at Nellis AFB. And I'm sorry to have to say this, but you are all under arrest."

6

"Good morning, ladies and gentlemen."

Emperor Daniel Sanders seated himself at the table in the conference room, surrounded by his top aides. They had been given complete authority over their respective departments and had been extremely busy the past few weeks, exhausting themselves in a dizzying attempt to carry out the emperor's orders. Now, it seemed, they had accomplished their tasks and had good news to report.

"Walters?" Sanders called. "Mr. Gerald Walters, Education Secretary, are you with us?"

"Yes, sir, sorry, sir," Walters stammered, putting away his phone. "The wife was just asking what I wanted for dinner."

"And?" Sanders asked, smiling. "What did you say?"

"I said that anything is fine with me."

Suddenly the room was filled with gasps and groans as the Cabinet members voiced their opinions.

"Wrong answer," Sanders said. "Let's just get to your report now."

Walters steeled himself as he prepared his oral presentation. He was the newest and youngest of the emperor's aides, but had just graduated with a Ph.D. in education, making him a clear appointment choice for Sanders.

"Well, sir," he cleared his throat, "the first thing that I did was to abolish the common education standards of the previous administration. I found the methods to be illogical and impractical. Students learn in a variety of ways and naturally excel in some areas but do more poorly in others. Forcing all students to excel in all areas is an abuse, and I am presently working to eradicate the grading system. For instance, someone with a knack for mathematics and sciences should not be shunned from pursuing engineering simply because they got a 'D' in history or a foreign language.

"Additionally, with the help of the Treasury Secretary, I am pleased to announce enormous pay increases for all faculty across the board. Our teachers deserve much more than what they have been earning, and it's a shame that in this country we give athletes and actors millions of dollars for two hours of entertainment. Thank you."

The Cabinet clapped in approval of Secretary Walter's report and achievements. The emperor, however, looked concerned.

"Educators are paid by either taxes or tuition. Where are these pay increases going to come from?"

James MacDonald, Secretary of the Treasury, raised his hand.

"I can answer that one, sir. We are proposing government funding of all education systems. All teachers would be paid government employees."

"So what you're saying," Sanders wondered, "is that all of our educators across the board are going to be on Uncle Sam's private payroll?"

"Not entirely," MacDonald explained. "It will trickle down. University faculty will be paid by the state, districts will be paid by the city or county, but we will have more money to provide to them, based on my restructuring plan.

"I am effectively eliminating standardized welfare and Social Security from the federal budget, as well as decreasing the budget for the military."

"I assume you and Defense Secretary Bright have worked out those details?"

"We have, sir," Michael Bright answered. "It will be in my report."

"So," MacDonald continued, "new federal standards for WIC and food stamps will be imposed and will be granted by request only. There will be no more organized federal or state food programs, only individual assistance.

"In addition, Social Security will be restructured. Presently, the SSA is a handout organization, effectively giving retirees money that their children are paying into. With the impending retirement of the baby boomers, and the skeleton workforce we have now making peanuts, there will be no money left. So, we will foot the bill for the rest of the current retirees for the next 10 years, and every penny that is put into the SSA by the current workforce will be theirs to keep when they retire.

"Here's where it gets good. I am personally writing new tax standards. Those businesses who produce at least 90% of their output within Uncle Sam's borders will get incredible tax breaks, and those who choose to continue most of their work overseas will receive a sticker shock every April 15. My favorite part is the huge tax breaks connected to big businesses that personally donate their resources – not just their money – but their time, their employees, and their food to local community projects for the homeless. No more just writing a check, but getting up close and seeing the other side. I call it 'incentivized socialism'."

"Rob from the rich and give to the poor, right?"

"Not quite, sir. Pure socialism is about governmental ownership and distribution of wealth until everyone is compensated equally. A fast food employee and a CEO make the same amount of money for different work. I won't steal anyone's money. I'll just make it worth their while to give their money away. It isn't the government's job to drive the car, but to just get the battery started and let the nation take over from there."

The Cabinet again announced their approval with a round of applause.

"Michael?" Sanders addressed the Defense Secretary. "Anything to add?"

"Yes, sir. Mr. MacDonald's plans involve the immediate recall of all troops in foreign lands, and I can't disagree with him. It is NOT our job to police the world. We can save a lot of money, a lot of long-distance angst for families, and not to mention a lot of lives by not having American troops overseas, especially in war zones. In fact, the UN Secretary General agrees with my position. If they're our allies, we don't need to be over there unless they're attacked. If they're not our allies, why are we there? This is America. Let them fight it out."

"Thank you, Michael," Sanders said as the applause died down.

"Lastly, let's hear from our Homeland Security Advisor. Keith?"

Keith Malcolm settled into his chair, looking around the table at everyone gathered, staring into their eyes.

"Sir," he began, "it is my duty to report uprisings from within our borders."

"My God," Sanders mumbled. "Foreign splinter cells?"

"No, sir," Malcolm answered. "American. There are a growing number of malcontents who are realizing that you haven't subdued an insurrection but have successfully staged one. Now, we are under martial law, and with the help of Secretary Bright we are recalling more troops to deal with the situation, but if public unrest reaches a pinnacle, I don't know that we're prepared for the consequences."

Sanders breathed a heavy sigh.

"Are you finished?"

"Just one more thing, sir. We all believe in you, and in this new government. This is what is best for our nation. I believe I echo everyone here when I say that is time to stop sticking our head in the Middle Eastern sand and start thinking about the Stars and Stripes. If we don't, there soon may not be a United States left, and it will be our own fault."

◆ ◆ ◆

The air was crisp as a cold wind blew across the Potomac River, sending Becky Larkin-Murray deeper into her trench coat. Her hand shook visibly as she gripped the microphone, silently running through her report in her mind.

"We are live in five, four, three, two…"

"Good morning, I am live here in Washington where I have just spoken with self-proclaimed emperor Daniel Sanders and his advisors. The staff has assured me that this dramatic shift in the government was in fact NOT a coup-de-tat, but rather a pre-emptive strike against a possible uprising by President Robert Stevens as well as most, if not all, of Capitol Hill, including Congressmen, congressional aides, lobbyists and all those involved in the Supreme Court. This sounded a bit far-fetched to me at first, but I was conveniently placated with alleged confession videos of all parties involved. Here are just a few of those closed-circuit confessions. You be the judge."

Becky's image was replaced by footage of an interrogation room. Homeland Security Director Keith Malcolm was seated across from a young-looking man with short, dark hair.

"What is your name?"
"Congressman Bill Coleman."
"What is your position in Washington?"
"I am currently serving my first two-year term in the House of Representatives."
"Are you aware of a secret plot to overthrow the current executive administration of the United States?"
"Yes."
"And are you in agreement with such an insurrection?"
"Yes."

The image was replaced by another interrogation by Director Malcolm, this time with a different suspect.

"What is your name?"
"Robert Stevens."
"What is your position in Washington?"
"I am Commander-in-Chief, the chief executive officer of the United States of America."

"Are you aware of a secret plot to overthrow the current executive administration of the United States?"

"Yes."

"And are you in agreement with such an insurrection?"

"Yes."

"Now these are just two of the hundreds of confession videos that were released to the media, but each one plays out the same four questions, and each ends with the same answer: 'Yes, I am in agreement to overthrow the government.' Live from Capitol Hill, this is Becky Larkin-Murray."

◆ ◆ ◆

Brian Murray sat on his favorite bar stool in Lou's Pub sipping a whiskey. He had just watched his wife's report on the government situation when his phone started to ring in his pocket. Lou looked at him with knowing eyes. Brian returned the gaze and grabbed his phone, only to realize that it wasn't Becky calling.

"Hello, dad."

"Hey, son, how are things going these days?"

"Well, let's see," Brian sneered. "Wow, what *has* happened in the last seven years since you contacted me?"

"Hey, sorry, I've been busy."

"Oh, yes, I forgot. The great Ted Murray, oil company CEO, has to take care of his two Mercedes and his Bentley."

"Okay, so I've had some priorities out of order, but I want to make it up to you."

"What are you talking about?"

"I heard you've run into a rough spot lately with employment, and I want you to come work for me. The people are good and the money's great. Becky won't even need to do that news thing anymore."

"First of all, Becky loves doing 'that news thing'. Second, the money may be great, but I can't say the same for the character of all the employees."

"Now you just hold on right there..."

"Besides," Brian interrupted, "your company is one of the reasons this nation is in bad shape. If people could afford their gas, maybe they wouldn't need cheap cars made in other countries, I would still have a job, and we wouldn't be having this discussion!"

Brian angrily hung up on his father, slamming his phone down on the bar. He looked up at Lou, who shot him a puzzled look.

"Family," he sighed.

◆ ◆ ◆

"Mrs. Elliot, did the mail come yet?"

"Yes, Mr. Whitman," Mrs. Elliot replied, handing him an official-looking envelope. "This just came for you."

Mr. Whitman entered his office, closing the door and opening his mail. What he read made him shake.

Dear Principal Whitman:

This is to advise you that Peabody High School, together with all of the other schools in your district, is to receive a substantial pay increase, effective immediately. Our office would like to personally applaud your efforts as educators and compensate you fairly for the service you provide to this nation's youth.

Additionally, you may regard the common education standards as null and void. Please educate our children as it best suits their abilities because, after all, education is about them, not us.

Once again, I wish to thank you for your service to our children. Please find enclosed a check for your school, to be spent on whatever programs you deem necessary. It's our way of saying, "Pay it forward to the next generation."

Sincerely,

Gerald Walters

Ed. Sec., USA

7

Everything was perfect that evening. The dining room table was decorated neatly from end-to-end, a colorful holiday cloth setting a backdrop for eight place settings and an even more colorful arrangement of foods: mashed potatoes, sweet potatoes, stuffing, cranberry sauce, gravy and a basketful of rolls.

Brian Murray seated himself between his kids and started to help himself to a large spoonful of sweet potatoes.

"Ahem," Becky rebuked, bringing out a roasted turkey from the kitchen. "Our guests have not arrived yet. You just put those back and hold your horses."

Brian obeyed with a smile as his wife set the 15 pound bird down between the potato bowls. Suddenly, the doorbell rang.

"It's only your folks," Brian called after her. "I'll just get the kids' plates ready."

"They're teenagers, Bri," Becky answered at the door. "They can wait and get their own when...everyone is here!"

Chief of Staff Richard Larkin and his wife Camille entered the dining room and took their seats at the table, giving warm smiles to their son-in-law and grandchildren.

"By the way, hon," Brian asked, "who are these extra plates for? Are we expecting..."

"Surprise!" Ted Murray shouted as he and Nancy walked into the room, carrying a pan of food.

"...my parents," Brian finished.

"I invited them over, dear," Becky explained. "They didn't hesitate for a second."

"We brought green bean casserole," Brian's mom announced. "Just the way you used to like it, with extra cream of mushroom soup."

"Fine," Brian said, looking at his wife. "Have a seat. Just don't expect any warm hugs."

Ted and Nancy seated themselves next to the Larkins, keeping a somewhat watchful eye on Richard. The Chief of Staff returned the gaze to Ted, seemingly sizing him up.

The turkey was carved and the dinner began to pass uneventfully as no one spoke a word to each other except for the occasional "pass the rolls". Then Becky's phone rang.

"Excuse me," she said, looking at the caller ID. "I need to take this in the kitchen."

The family quietly returned to their food, Ted and Richard still eying one another warily.

"So, kids," Nancy Murray broke the silence, "Nana wants to know. How's school been going?"

"Great," Heather, Brian's daughter, replied. "Principal Whitman just got a letter and a check from the government and the band got all new instruments."

"Our principal got a check, too," one of the twin boys said. "We got new desks in our classrooms."

"That's wonderful, son," Brian said. "Instruments for the high school and desks for the elementary. And all on the government's dime?"

"Like it's *their* money," Ted grumbled. "I pay good taxes for those."

"I'm, uh..." Larkin began, leaving the table. "I'm gonna go see if Becky's okay."

"Keep your political comments to yourself, dad," Brian threatened. "Becky's father just so happens to be the second-in-command of this nation."

"Oh, I know exactly who he is, son. He's a backstabbing, cutthroat pencil-pusher who wants to see 'good enterprise' suffer and give charity to people who are just going to use it on drugs and killing."

Brian was astonished.

"I'm just gonna go help Rick," Camille stated.

"What are you talking about, dad?" Brian asked when Mrs. Larkin had left.

"Remember that job I offered you? Well, the offer is rescinded because the job is gone. I had to cut back in a number of areas because your wonderful father-in-law took over the government and decided to play socialist. Now most of my money has to go to Americans, either by payroll or charity. With rising costs, I simply can't afford to keep some that I have, let alone new hires."

"Well," Brian replied, "first of all, I still wouldn't work for your greedy capitalism enterprise, and second, it doesn't matter, because my old employer brought back the automotive industry to our little city, and I have my old job back. Something about 'incentivized socialism'. Build America, for America."

"Don't buy into it, son, I'm telling you. 'Incentivized socialism' going to drive this nation into its grave."

❖ ❖ ❖

"Why the hell did I just see the Chief of Staff's daughter on the news when she was forbidden not to?"

"I know, Bruce," Becky replied as her parents entered the kitchen behind her.

"You know," Channel 6 News Chief Bruce Barnes said gruffly on the other end. *"Well, did you know, Mrs. Ace Reporter, that I've got leads on stories speculating that you're in on the whole plot to destroy the government? Did you know that there are civil insurgent groups forming, and your name is at the top of their kill list? I warned you this could happen. You have just made an enemy of Mr. Red-blooded American and you had better prove you're not a terrorist, and fast."*

"And just how am I supposed to do that?"

"We have an anonymous tipster in Nevada who says he's seen what's really been going on, says the President and the rest of our 'traitors' have been detained in a facility out there. Go get some answers, Beck, for your sake and for mine."

"Question, chief."

"Shoot."

"Does our source say who helped to coordinate all this?"

"Of course he did," the news chief replied as Becky turned to see her father standing behind her. *"It was daddy dearest."*

❖ ❖ ❖

"Okay, thanks Mr. Barnes."

Sgt. Jonathan Sanders hung up the pay phone just beyond the barracks and ran to rejoin Sgt. Chris Jenkins, his best friend and combat partner.

"Boy, you're really asking for it, aren't you?" Chris joked.

"I have to do the right thing," Sanders replied. "I know what's really going on here, and something has to be done."

"To stop your father, you mean? Johnny, what part of 'not in his will' don't you understand?"

"And what part of the military oath didn't *you* understand? We have a duty to freedom, loyalty and the truth."

"The truth?" Chris laughed. "Didn't you see those confession videos?"

"Yes, I did," Johnny replied. "I also happened to see an entirely different story go down. I'm telling you, my father is not to be trusted, and I personally know of at least fifteen groups of insurgents around the country who feel the same way. They're just waiting on someone to take the lead and rise up to reclaim our nation."

◆ ◆ ◆

"All right, gentlemen, let's make this quick so we can go home to our families. I'm sorry to do this on Thanksgiving, but I need to get some updates on our national state. Treasury?"

"The Treasury," James MacDonald began, "is happy to announce a 75% resurgence of industrial jobs across the country, including factories that have long since been abandoned. Products, it seems, are once again being made in the United States."

"Thank you, Secretary MacDonald. Education?"

"Yes, Your Highness," Gerald Walters replied. "Education Department reports a significant increase in testing results and a dramatic segregation of skills in classrooms. We now know which kids are better at which subjects through simple implementation and observation of the new education standards. Additionally, schools report a higher concentration rate, lower instances of bullying and an overall boost in morale as a result of individualized attention and money for more projects. The income generated by business charities in Mr. MacDonald's 'incentivized socialism' plan seems to be working. A stroke of genius."

"Very good," Sanders said. "Defense?"

"All troops are home and enjoying wonderful holidays with their loved ones across the nation."

"Awesome, and Homeland? How are our citizens treating us, Keith?"

Keith Malcolm gulped as he began to report his findings.

"We have now identified over 20 cluster groups of American insurgents. They are all isolated from one another, but there seems to be increasing communication from one group in particular, and we believe this to be the base of the ringleader."

"Where is this base located, Keith?"

Keith swallowed hard and took a deep breath as he looked Emperor Sanders in the eye. They both knew who was in this area, in this group and who was possibly leading the rebellion.

"Your Highness," he managed, "the base is located in Nevada."

❖ ❖ ❖

Becky Larkin walked briskly in the chilly, Nevada night, hunkering down close to the shadows to avoid being seen. She crept around one building, then another, until she reached a dimly lit alleyway with yellow paint markings. This was the spot. This is where the informant would meet her.

She glanced at her watch. 11:05. Five minutes late. Never had she had a source show up late before, although she never had a source meet her this late at night before. She moved to check her watch again when immediately something hit her in the back, knocking her to the ground.

A warm, gloved hand quickly covered her mouth as wet lips pressed against her ear lobe.

"Don't scream, lady. Just listen carefully and you'll be safe."

Panic-stricken, Becky silently nodded her head in agreement. Suddenly, the hand that had clamped her mouth shut now helped her to her feet, leading her further back into the alley.

"I'm your source," the assailant whispered calmly. "My name is Johnny, and that's all the name you're getting."

"Johnny?" Becky asked. "As in, Staff Sergeant Jonathan Sanders, son of Emperor Daniel Sanders, stationed here at Nellis AFB in Nevada?"

"Who told you?" Johnny demanded, coming out of the darkness.

"I'm a reporter, kid. No one told me. Now what's the scoop?"

Johnny cautiously moved further out of the alleyway and peered around the wall. Looking both ways, he reached back and grabbed Becky's hand, pulling her quickly toward a large hangar door. He grabbed his military ID, again checking around him, and swiped his badge at a PIN console, unlocking the hangar with a green light and a beep.

As he opened the door, Becky gasped. Filling the hangar were hundreds of metal bunkbeds, and in those beds sat most of the nation's elected leaders, including President Robert Stevens, who stepped forward for introductions.

"Mrs. Becky Larkin, this is President Robert Stevens. President Stevens, news reporter Becky Larkin."

"Yeah," Stevens said, "you're Rick's daughter. I suppose you're here to uncover the truth about what happened in Washington and help restore things to their rightful order, huh?"

"That's my goal, yes, sir."

"Well, forget it."

"Sir?"

"Everybody's saying one thing or another, right?"

"Yes, sir," Becky replied.

"Some say that Sanders is a jackass – no offense, Johnny – and he took over the government and locked Capitol Hill away."

"Yes, sir," Johnny said. "I saw that with my own two eyes. I was in the Oval Office, remember? And no offense taken. My father *is* a jackass."

"Okay, well the other side is that we're all traitors who confessed to a conspiracy we were about to commit, true?"

"I reviewed those tapes myself, Mr. President," Becky answered. "Pretty incriminating, although I still retain my objectivity. I have a feeling you have some answers."

"Well, yes," President Stevens replied, leaning in close, "but first you two have to promise to go off the record on this one, not breathing a word about this to anyone, not even the Senators in here."

"Agreed," Johnny and Becky said.

"Good," the President smiled. "Now, listen closely. What if, this time, there were *three* sides to a story?"

8

"He said what?!"

News Channel 6 director Bruce Barnes was currently in a meeting with his ace reporter, Becky Larkin-Murray. She had just come from an exclusive interview with Robert Stevens, the now-deposed President of the United States. She returned with a very intriguing story.

"Do you realize what this means?" he shouted.

"Yes, sir, I do," Becky replied, "but do you realize that I'm under strict orders not to publicly disclose any of this?"

Bruce was visibly agitated.

"Beck, if what you're telling me is true, then this is the single-most top story in the history of news broadcasts. Can you verify any of this?"

"I can, but as I said, not at this time."

"What are you waiting for, the return of Christ?" Bruce demanded. "This country is going insane. People are taking sides for and against the new government."

"People have always taken sides, Bruce," Becky answered.

"Not like this," he explained. "Factions are taking up arms against each other. Waging war. It's like the 1860's all over again. Brother versus brother."

"I understand, Bruce, but this is strictly off the record. The President knows what he's doing, I'm sure of it."

A knock on the door interrupted their meeting.

"Who is it?"

"Just Peter," came the voice from the other side of the glass. He quickly opened the door and scurried into the conference room.

"Sir," he said, out of breath. "There's a protest going on at the White House grounds. Something about 'Occupy Capitol Hill'. I think it could get ugly."

"More lower middle class?"

"No, sir. It's actually white collar. Corporate CEOs and such."

Bruce looked at his two top reporters.

"Okay, Becky, you're up."

"But sir," Peter cried, "I had to take her senile baker story!"

"I'm sure she's sorry about that," Bruce replied, glaring at Becky, "but this is her scoop now, and I trust that she'll know how to handle it and do the right thing. Especially since things are getting out of hand?"

"Yes, sir," Becky answered as she left the room. "And for what it's worth, Bruce, you were right. The madness has to stop."

◆ ◆ ◆

President Stevens paced the floor of the hangar that currently served as the brig for him and the rest of the government "conspirators". He had received an anonymous tip that a friend would be along to help them very soon, but so far nothing out of the ordinary had happened.

A few of the Congressmen had gotten together a poker game and were currently laughing and carrying on, which was no small feat considering they had been at each other's throats about gun control and immigration just a few short weeks ago.

Some other Senators were working together on a plan of escape, just in case the tip they had received turned out to be bogus. They had even enlisted the help of a lobbyist who had some experience in the construction industry. There was some animated discussion for a while about whose plan was the best, but had decided in the end to blend all the ideas together.

Suddenly, the hangar door opened, and Sgt. Jenkins and Sgt. Sanders stepped in.

"Okay, everyone," Jenkins yelled, "it's 2300 hours. That means lights out."

"So that," Sanders added in a softer voice, "we can get you all out of here under the cover of darkness."

The entire bay erupted in a quiet applause as the two officers worked quickly to usher everyone out of the hangar and off the base.

"I bet you feel a little like Moses, don't you, son?" Stevens asked Sgt. Sanders.

"Sir?"

"You know, leading us out of slavery and into the desert at night."

"Oh, I suppose so, sir," Sanders chuckled. "Now you said you had a rendezvous waiting for your entire party?"

"Yep, it's all settled. He has an entire fleet of helicopters and Humvees ready to pick us up and get us out of here undetected."

"Incredible," Sanders replied. "I'm glad he's on your side, or our side, or whatever side anyone's on anymore. Your story is so confusing."

"Shhh," Stevens whispered, looking behind them at the others. "They're not in on our little secret just yet. It's better that way."

"Oh, right, sorry," Sanders apologized. "So, I was wondering, exactly who *does* know the real story?"

"Well," the president answered as they approached their rendezvous party. "Me and the others I mentioned in my interview, then there's you and that reporter, of course, and lastly there's him."

Stevens pointed to a young, black-haired man who approached the large escape crowd.

"Everything ready to go, Bill?" the president asked.

"Yes, sir, Mr. President," Bill replied. "I've got amphibians, armored personnel vehicles, Apache choppers and even a few Sherman tanks for the less claustrophobic. We'll get everyone out of here safely and smoothly, and completely off the radar. My special touch."

"Good to hear," Stevens said. "Oh, Bill, this is Sgt. Jonathan Sanders, Daniel's son. He helped us get off the base."

"Pleasure to meet you, Sgt.," Bill said, offering his hand. "I'm Senator Bill Coleman."

◆ ◆ ◆

As Becky Larkin-Murray pulled up to 1600 Pennsylvania that afternoon, the news van was pummeled by protestors holding signs and yelling obscene things about the media and about government. She quickly pulled over to an adjacent street and made her way back to the mob scene.

Everywhere she looked there were businessmen and women with placards that read, "Government Stay Out Of Our Pockets", "Big Brother Is Wrong For Big Business", and "Down With Socialism". The mob was shouting and had even begun to riot. Washington police were on the scene to handle crowd control, but it looked like a losing battle. The SWAT team even had trucks parked down the street, ready to strike if necessary.

Becky cautiously made her way up to the scene, flashing her press badge to the local authorities to gain access. As she neared the protestors, she saw right away who she intended to interview.

"Mr. Murray?" she called to her father-in-law. "Ted Murray! It's Becky."

"Becky!" he called, rushing over. "This is too dangerous a place for you to be right now. Go home to Brian and the kids."

"Sorry, pop," she replied, pointing at her cameraman, "but I have a job to do, and I'm pretty sure you want your voice heard around the nation."

"You're right," Ted said. "I want Washington to know what kind of a pig-headed ploy this is. It's bad enough that the Vice President has somehow made himself Emperor and turned our democracy into a travesty, but now he's gone and ruined the economy in the process. He calls it 'incentivized socialism'. Make it worth our while to give all of our profits away to some homeless punk who won't put in a decent day's work for his own money. Thievery in its highest form is still thievery."

"What about those who say that the Emperor has helped them financially? As a matter of fact, my children just saw a substantial shift in the funding and in the entire teaching system at their school. And, as I recall, your son just received his auto manufacturing job back after the company closed its plant overseas and relocated back to the States, a directive initiated by Emperor Sanders. I suppose it's all in how you look at it."

"I would choose my words carefully around here, *Mrs. Larkin*. I need not remind you of your relationship with a certain government official."

"My father has nothing to do with this, Mr. Murray. Can't you see that the new reforms have been good for us?"

"Maybe for one small family in Happytown, USA, but you're not seeing the big picture. These reforms will have a ripple effect which will destroy the entire economic structure of the nation."

"What's coming will benefit the nation in ways you could never conceive of," Becky retorted.

"How do you know what's coming?" Ted asked, eying her curiously. "You know something, don't you?"

◆ ◆ ◆

"Those protestors were rough today, dear," Candice Stevens said, climbing into bed.

"Yeah, but the police were able to maintain control," Emperor Sanders answered, peeking out of the bedroom window at the empty front lawn. "They're all gone now, that's the main thing."

Sanders slid into bed next to the First Lady and sighed.

"How long can we keep it up?" he wondered aloud.

"Your record is about half an hour," Candice replied.

"No, no, I mean this whole thing."

"You mean 'us'?"

"No, the takeover, the government, the reforms, the policies."

"As long as it takes. People will see it your way eventually. It's for the good of the nation."

"Do you think anyone suspects?"

"I don't think so."

"What about Robert?" Sanders worried.

"Honey, Robert knows about it, remember?"

"I know, but I mean, what if he tells someone? If it's not handled correctly and at the right time, this entire thing could blow up."

"Look, he knows what he's doing," Candice comforted. "I'm sure no one else knows what's going on."

9

"What is *he* doing here?" one of the senators asked, leaning over the back seat of an Apache chopper and staring at Senator Bill Coleman.

"He's helping us escape," Stevens answered. He and the rest of Capitol Hill, along with Sgt. Jonathan Sanders and Sgt. Chris Jenkins, were making their way out of the Nevada desert where they had been held captive for a number of weeks. They were on their way to the White House to confront self-proclaimed Emperor Daniel Sanders and reclaim the Presidency.

"But he died," the senator continued, "I watched him die."

"Ah, the sacrifice," Coleman explained. "You know, no one actually *saw* me die. And besides, no electromagnet on the planet could do that much bodily damage."

"But your hand…"

Coleman raised up his arms and showed them to his fellow senator. His skin was completely healthy.

"Black magic marker washes off pretty easily."

"But why, then? Why the whole charade?"

"Well," Coleman started, "it's because…because…"

"Because you needed something to agree on," Stevens finished. "What better way to get four political parties to work together on something than to rally around a sacrifice?"

"So this was a ruse? Just to get us to play nice in the sandbox with each other?"

"Something like that."

"Then was it all a lie?" the senator continued. "I mean, were we even in any danger from radiation? Senator Haskins is still alive, isn't she?"

Stevens took a deep breath.

"Yes."

"Mr. President," the senator asked, "answer me this – were we actually locked up in that bunker?"

Stevens said nothing, silently looking ahead at the night sky through the windshield of the Apache.

"Better sit back, senator," Coleman said. "It could be a bumpy ride to Washington."

◆ ◆ ◆

Emperor Daniel Sanders seated himself at the head of the conference table and looked around the room at his advisors. All of the department heads wore smiles on their faces, seeming eager to give updates on their respective fields.

"Mr. MacDonald," Sanders began, "would you be so kind as to start us off with the economic report?"

"Gladly, sir," replied the treasury secretary. "The latest financial analysis would indicate healthy growth in the employment sector, as well as an overall increase in private revenues. Businesses are thriving once again – including small businesses – and America is getting back to work. An estimated 85% of industries that have outsourced their manufacturing overseas have now returned most of their production to the United States, boosting the Gross National Product and helping to dig the country out of debt.

"Health care is also less of a concern now that we have stopped trying to regulate and own it. Private citizens now have the freedom to choose insurance or not, and non-profits have sprung up across the nation and offered to foot the bill for many out-of-pocket expenses.

"Oil production is at an all-time high now that we have begun to use our own oil fields in the north-northwest region of the country. Companies are getting out of the Middle East and starting to reap the benefits of domestic profits.

"The country is healing itself, sir; all we needed to do was get the ball rolling. We have virtually eliminated the greed that is inherent in capitalism and replaced it with compassion. We rid ourselves of 'Welfare' and instead promoted the general welfare of the people."

"Good to hear," Sanders praised. "Mr. Walters?"

"Yes, sir," the education secretary replied. "Great news to report. Now that standardized grading and scoring have been eliminated, and since we have focused on the talents and abilities of the individual student, we have seen dramatic social and technical improvements. People are no longer working jobs they hate, but are rather redirected into more fulfilling careers they absolutely love. They are thriving in those fields because not only are we allowing them to do so, but also granting them the resources and encouragement they need to succeed. By our estimates, the entire nation will be 'doing what they love' in the next decade or so. Morale will improve drastically, and I believe we will see the return of trust in the government and an overall renewed sense of patriotism."

"Wonderful, wonderful. And speaking of patriotism, how are we doing on that front, Mr. Malcolm?"

Homeland Secretary Keith Malcolm cleared his throat.

"Well, sir, for the most part, we have seen a significant drop in rebellions and insurrections. The American people are starting to realize that the new administration is *not* trying to own their wallets or anything about their lives. As Secretary Walters explained, patriotism *is* beginning to return, almost to a point not seen since WWII. We have once again given hope to the nation. In fact, there is only one faction that has yet to surrender to the empire."

"Only one?" Sanders wondered. "Who are they? What do they want?"

"It's the President and Congress," Malcolm admitted. "Word is they have your son and his friend with them as hostages. Last reports indicated they were headed for Washington, and they were looking for you."

◆ ◆ ◆

"So *what* exactly is going on?" Brian Murray asked his wife as he dried a spoon.

"I told you, I'm not allowed to say," Becky answered, scraping spaghetti from a plate.

"But this all has to do with Emperor Sanders and President Stevens, right?"

"Yes, and that's all I'll tell you."

"Even if I ask nicely?" Brian said, shooting Becky a sad face. "Pretty please?"

"Okay, fine," she caved. "Well, you know how there are always two sides to every story? Like, either Sanders is a power-hungry dictator or Stevens was really trying to take control and Sanders stopped him? Well, this time there are three sides. It would seem that Stevens and Sanders…"

Ding-dong!

"I'll get it," Becky volunteered, ignoring her husband's frustrated growl.

She opened the door to find Ted Murray on the other side.

"Can I come in?"

"Of course, Ted," Becky replied. "Brian, your dad's here."

Brian came into the living room as Ted was shedding his jacket. He gave his father a look that spoke volumes.

"What are you doing here?"

"I came to see you," Ted answered. "I've been doing a lot of thinking recently, and I realized that life is too short to be an old miser. The Emperor is right. The only way this nation will be vibrant once again is if we all pitch in and do our part. There are people who don't have, and I have more than enough to share. So, I took a hit on the bottom line, brought production back to the U.S., and umm….liquidated some assets."

"Assets?"

"I sold the mansion and the lake house, in addition to the Bentley and the Rolls."

"What?"

"Your mother and I found a great little brick ranch home in the country, and we're driving a used pick-up, manufactured right here in America. Thought you'd appreciate that."

"Just a couple weeks ago you were ready to kill Sanders with your bare hands. Why the sudden change of heart?"

"Well, let's just say your wife can be very convincing, even if the story is a bit far-fetched."

Brian looked at Becky, a light bulb switching on in his head.

"You told my father before me?"

"Honey, you don't understand. It was at the protest. I had to say something."

"Well, whatever it is, it must be really good," Brian said gruffly. "So, as I was saying, what exactly is going on?"

◆ ◆ ◆

An Apache chopper landed directly on the White House lawn as Sherman tanks and other armored vehicles converged on 1600 Pennsylvania Avenue. Immediately, secret service personnel rushed from the building firing weapons, but were no match for the trained squadrons that Senator Coleman had rallied together. A swarm of Navy Seals and Delta Force fighters quickly took to combat, subduing the men in black and granting the president access to his former home.

"We'll take it from here, gentlemen," Coleman ordered. "Set up a perimeter and engage as needed. Wait for further instructions."

President Stevens and Bill Coleman entered the White House just behind Sgt. Jonathan Sanders, who peered around every corner until it was safe to give the "all-clear". The three men quickly made their way to the Oval Office, where the emperor and his staff appeared to be waiting on them.

"What took you boys so long?" he asked with a chuckle.

"Daniel Sanders," his son managed, "I'm placing you under arrest."

"On what grounds, son?"

"On uh...on ummm....on..."

"On high treason and conspiracy to subdue the government of the United States of America," Stevens finished.

"Well, then," Sanders said, "it looks like you got me."

"Horse hockey!" Richard Larkin protested. "Dan, these men are the criminals. We have their confessions on tape, remember?"

"Chill out, Rick," Sanders replied. "I'll be back before you know it."

Emperor Daniel Sanders approached the three men with his arms held out.

"Okay, boys, let's get this over with."

10

Daniel Sanders awoke with a start as a heavy steel door clanked open. He sat up on his hard, concrete bed and rubbed the sleep out of his eyes. A faint light shone through a small window embedded high up on the wall, revealing the first glimpses of the break of day.

He'd been here all night, tossing and turning on an unforgiving mattress. His hair was a mess, his clothes wrinkled and disheveled. He stood up, stretched his arms and walked over to the door to greet his visitor.

"Looks like you won, Mr. President," he said, holding out his hand.

"I suppose I did," President Stevens said, giving Sanders a firm handshake. "But don't think I haven't overlooked what you've managed to accomplish. I mean, the economy is booming once again. We're poised to eliminate our debt in the next ten years, the military is back home where they belong, and don't even get me started about your education reforms. Brilliant work, I would say."

"Thank you, sir, but you did even better, if I may say so. I mean, getting Congress to work together and forget party politics? Convincing them that I was actually a bad guy? Stroke of genius."

"Hey, you managed to convince the Cabinet to 'overthrow' the administration," Stevens laughed.

"Speaking of which – shouldn't they be in trouble for conspiracy?"

"We'll work that all out. In the meantime, I'll go file some paperwork and sign a pardon for you. You'll be home this afternoon, I'm sure."

"Thanks, Bob," Sanders replied, patting the president's shoulder.

"Oh, and one more thing," Stevens said, turning around. In one move he balled up his fist and punched his Vice President across the jaw, sending him falling backwards onto the hard cement bunk.

"Don't ever touch my wife again."

◆ ◆ ◆

"Lead anchor? Staying here at the station and reporting from behind a desk? I don't know what to say."

"Say 'Yes, Bruce, thank you for my promotion and raise'."

"Yes, Bruce," Becky Murray replied. "Thank you for my promotion and raise."

"You're welcome, kiddo," Bruce said. "You've earned it. There's just one catch."

"I figured as much."

"I need you to cover one last field story."

"What and where is it?"

"Take a wild guess."

"Washington?"

"How did you ever guess that?" Bruce smiled. "The White House is calling a press conference about a recent turn of events, which I'm guessing has to do with that little story you told me. Go get me that scoop, Beck."

"Will do, sir," Becky answered. "And thank you again."

◆ ◆ ◆

Sgt. Jonathan Sanders sat shaking his legs and tapping his feet, visibly excited. He was seated next to his best friend, Sgt. Christopher Jenkins, behind a podium on a stage in front of hundreds of his army buddies and certain military brass. His CO, Colonel William Overton, was addressing the audience about the bravery of these two men despite the orders of their superiors.

"And so," he was saying, "we can learn a lot from these men, who chose to do what was right and defy orders when something seemed amiss. With that, I would like to present the Medal of Valor to Sergeants Christopher Jenkins and Jonathan Sanders."

The room erupted in applause as Jenkins and Sanders stood front and center on stage to receive their awards.

"Thank you, son," Overton said as he pinned the badge on Jenkins.

"Thank you, sir."

"Thank you, son," Overton repeated to Sanders. "You're one fine officer, and I understand there's even a bump up to 1ˢᵗ Sergeant in the works."

"Sir? A promotion?"

"Let's just say you've gone above and beyond the call of duty, and we need more men like you."

◆ ◆ ◆

The White House press room was abuzz with activity. Reporters from the Times, the Globe-Democrat, and the Herald took front seats, scrambling to get their questions out first after the press secretary had finished his statements. Becky Murray took a seat near the middle, smiling. She had advanced knowledge of what was about to happen, and it was almost guaranteed that her father, the second-in-command of the American Empire, would give her an exclusive interview.

"Good evening, ladies and gentlemen of the press," the secretary began. "I have just been briefed on the status of President Stevens and Emperor Daniel Sanders, as well as on the State of the Union. As it stands, I am not allowed to speak on either gentlemen's behalf, so I will now surrender the floor to Robert Stevens, President of the United States."

The press room went berserk as President Stevens stepped out from behind a door and onto the stage in front of the media.

"Please, be seated," he said as he took the podium. "I have explanations and answers for every single one of you, just be patient with me.

"First of all, let me say that my health has not been deteriorating, nor have I technically been imprisoned for the last two months. I, along with the members of Capitol Hill, have been on a sort of hiatus from the nation, secluded away in an isolated bunker in Nevada, more commonly referred to as 'Area 51'. While there, we put aside party politics and worked together to 'escape'. The fact that we were not actually locked away was known only to myself, Senator William Coleman and Emperor Daniel Sanders."

The media was in an uproar as Senator Coleman and Emperor Sanders appeared on stage, joining the president.

"Calm down, everyone, and let me explain. As you might have figured out, there was no government takeover. It was all set up, a ruse of sorts. Daniel appeared to legitimately force me out of office and then dissolve the other two branches of government. With his newfound position and power, he was able to decisively enact some much-needed reforms into some outdated systems.

"Meanwhile, I was able to work with the members of Congress, re-introducing them to teamwork and goal-setting. They learned to adapt quickly and painlessly, and have even begun forming new friendships across party lines.

"So, in summary, the government has recreated the infrastructure of the nation and given power back to the American people, and the government will continue to act as it was designed to by the founding fathers – to exist only in the case of emergencies. As Abraham Lincoln once stated, America is a nation created by the people and for the people. The Empire will cease to exist, and the United States will be reborn as she was meant to be. We will continue to reform as needed, but only in the interests of the nation as a whole, and not solely for the benefit of the federal government.

"A hundred years ago this nation was great. Then over time the government was given too much responsibility in caring for the nation. No more. This is *your* country. Buy. Sell. Travel. Revive the great American spirit within you and don't worry about Big Brother watching you anymore. Be the Americans you were born to be. Thank you, and may God Bless America."

ABOUT THE AUTHOR

Max Christian

I am a relatively new author, but I have been writing for years, supported by my wife of 13 years, 5 children and a loving bassethound.

www.ingramcontent.com/pod-product-compliance
Lightning Source LLC
Chambersburg PA
CBHW051715250726
48653CB00007B/3046